T0159130

A Guide to
Ethical Practices
in the
United States
Tax Industry

Terrence E. Simon, Ph.D.

Order this book online at www.trafford.com
or email orders@trafford.com

Most Trafford titles are also available at major online book retailers.

Cover Illustrated by: Marcus R. Embry
marcusrembry@gmail.com

Edited by: Sharlin Espinal
clwriting7@gmail.com

Printed in the United States of America.

ISBN: 978-1-4907-1696-1 (sc)
ISBN: 978-1-4907-1697-8 (e)

Trafford rev. 10/18/2013

 www.trafford.com

North America & international
toll-free: 1 888 232 4444 (USA & Canada)
fax: 812 355 4082

DEDICATION

To all clients who entrusted the preparation of
their tax returns to practitioners whose actions
resulted in harm, audits, payments of penalties and
interest, and a bad tax preparation experience.

ACKNOWLEDGMENTS

The completion of the book was not only by long demanding hours of work on my part, but by the support of my wife, children, family members, and friends. Thank you very much from the bottom of my heart for the invaluable support and advice given to me throughout the writing of the book.

TABLE OF CONTENTS

PREFACE

It is a commonly known fact among the tax practitioner community that ethical dilemmas are faced every day and affect interactions with clients. This state of affairs means that tax practitioners are used to navigating murky ethical waters in service to their work. If the issue of ethics was not complex enough, tax practitioners differ in culture, standards, and philosophy. Delving into these ethical dilemmas and cultural differences became a personal endeavor to me over the course of my scholarship on the topic.

Some may argue that current ethics and professional standards amongst the community are appropriate. But due to the great variance in education and training in the tax practitioner community this is not always the case.

In the United States, the tax practitioner can subscribe himself to several different ideologies. Each camp argues its merits and proposes a view of tax preparation that navigates the inconsistencies that many face. Idealists, Relativists, and Realists expound the virtues of their positions. But is one approach more correct?

The conflicting approaches to addressing ethical behavior is rooted in the customs and culture of the tax practitioner and his individual values, work background, age, and personality. Some scholars feel that organizational factors including management philosophy, job dimensions, competition, and economic conditions also influence the ethical behavior of tax practitioners.

Training is also often overlooked and much maligned by the community. In my research on this topic my endeavors resulted in *Reducing income tax preparation errors: An exploratory study of tax practitioners perceptions of training and Its Impact on income tax preparation*, a dissertation published in 2012. What I found is that many practitioners felt the issue was still a grave concern and garnered little to no attention in the community and among the governing bodies. Returning to training, I found that one of the most important factors in reducing the number and severity of unintentional errors is the level and effectiveness of that individual training. The pressure of satisfying a client's desire for a larger refund and the potential lack of knowledge regarding laws and procedure and the low likelihood of error detection creates a perfect storm for potential malpractice and abuse of the system.

INTRODUCTION

This book takes a position, one that has been reasoned through many years of tax practice in New York City and numerous conversations with other tax practitioners, that a baseline of ethical standards and policy changes are needed for the continued health and stability of the tax industry. The first section of this book highlights the need for and the promotion of an ethical culture in tax preparation. The second section discusses the ideologies of tax practitioners and how their beliefs shape practice. The third section analyses the pitfalls of tax practice and sheds light on the audit lottery. In the final section, strategies to prevent malpractice through training and education are explored.

It is my hope that through my roles as practitioner, administrator, and researcher I can impart lessons learned over a decade of experience and study into the field. If you are a tax practitioner starting out in the field, the lessons learned provide valuable starting points that will enhance your skills and competence in tax preparation while advising you on adhering to ethical standards. For clients, this book provides valuable insights into the operation of the IRS, adherence to the IRC, and the role of the tax practitioner in the tax preparation process.

Throughout the 19th and 20th centuries and in contemporary times, scholars and lawmakers continue to address the self-seeking indiscretions of individuals involved in business. First, the stock market crash of 1929 led to the formation of the Securities Exchange Commission (SEC). Second, the Lockheed scandal resulted in the Foreign Corrupt Practices Act of 1977. Third, the US Sentencing Guidelines of 1991 mitigate penalties dependent upon the ethical processes and procedures that corporations have in place to attempt to ensure the organization maintains ethical business practices. Finally, the corporate scandals involving Enron and other prominent corporations have led to the Sarbanes-Oxley Act of 2002.

Individuals and businesses that disregard business ethics responsibilities risk the danger of sanctions, penalties, and imprisonment. The tax preparation community is not immune from the risk associated with disregard for business ethics. While tax practitioners provide unique opportunities to affect the behaviors of clients, help them comply with tax laws, and meet their commitment to filing tax returns, they have a duty to adhere to professional standards and follow the law in the preparation of tax returns in their respective states.

There are several challenges facing the tax preparation community. The numbers of dishonest clients who intentionally understate income or overstate deductions are growing at astounding rates, as are those who are averse to compliance with tax laws. Additionally, recent research has shown there is an increasing number of unscrupulous tax practitioners who exploit loopholes in the Internal Revenue Code (IRC) leading clients into noncompliance with the aim of avoiding tax liabilities or getting larger refunds. However, the greatest challenge is the vast number of unregulated tax practitioners with little training, skills, and competence in tax preparation. To foster some level of skill and competence in tax preparation, tax practitioners must operate within a set framework of laws to avoid the risk of malpractice and a discussion of ethical standards and behavior is necessitated to establish a baseline for tax practitioners' professional responsibility to the wider tax community.

AN OVERVIEW OF THE
US TAX INDUSTRY

The Internal Revenue Service (IRS) is responsible for the administration of taxation in the United States. The IRS is a bureau of the United States Department of Treasury and is organized to carry out some aspects of the responsibilities of the Treasury Secretary. Often cited as a model of efficiency in tax administration globally, the IRS processed 237 million tax returns and collected approximately $2.5 trillion in 2012. In fact, $0.40 spent to collect every $100 in 2012 is impressive. The cost of collecting revenue is likely to decrease if the current trend continues.

The statistics above highlight the apparent efficient operation of the IRS but shed little light on the administration of taxation in the US. What it fails to highlight is the collaboration the IRS enjoys with several other state and local tax agencies, consumer affairs departments, employers, tax advocates, and not-for-profit organizations to carry out its mandate. The efficiency claimed by the IRS is somewhat misleading due to the fact that the work of many effective tax preparation organizations is credited to them.

The statistics also do not highlight the ethical deficiencies and policy issues of the U.S tax industry. Enshrined in the mission of the IRS is the belief that all clients deserve quality service. Although the IRS sets the standards of practice for the US tax industry, there are several stakeholders in the tax community with the responsibility to ensure that all clients have the best tax preparation experience. First, clients must take responsibility for the timely preparation and filing of tax returns in compliance with the Internal Revenue Code (IRC). Second, tax practitioners must exhibit high ethical standards of conduct while interfacing with other stakeholders in the tax community. Finally, the IRS role as enforcers of the IRC must escalate to meet the challenges of tax preparation in the 21st century.

In meeting the challenges of providing the best quality of service to clients, the IRS and tax practitioners encounter three major issues. First, the fact the 54% of all tax practitioners in the U.S. are unregulated is astonishing. Second, the annual audit rate of all income tax returns filed is 1%, a figure which researchers and practitioners alike feel set the tone for malpractice. And third, little is done to highlight the dilemmas or protect clients who are the real victims when the systems within the IRS and practices of tax practitioners fail.

The issues mentioned above should be addressed by local and state elected officials and lawmakers in Congress. The 1% audit rate and 54% unregulated tax practitioners are major policy weaknesses in the U.S tax industry.

Additionally, any system that fails to provide safety nets for its citizens who can be easily harmed by weak policies needs an act or acts of Congress to remedy the shortcoming. An in depth analysis and discussion of the policy weaknesses that lead to ethical deficiencies and malpractice in the U.S. tax industry is warranted because of these issues.

PART 1

Promoting an Ethical Culture in Tax Preparation

The tax preparation profession is a function of its tax practitioners and their performances in tax preparation. If tax practitioners fail to maintain standards in their practices, the profession falls into disrepute. This is beyond dispute. The effectiveness of the internal and external mechanisms established to maintain this high level of professionalism, however, remains to be seen. In order to understand how practitioners are held to standards, a bit of history is needed to give us context.

The IRS established guidelines to protect the income tax profession through Circular 230 to guarantee that tax practitioners are held to standards commensurate with the demands of the income tax community. Circular 230 was designed to promote ethical practice among tax practitioners, re-establish public confidence in the work of tax practitioners, and advocate best practice in providing tax advice. When Circular 230 was first introduced in 1940, tax practitioners were required to prepare accurate tax returns containing complete and relevant facts. As a consequence Circular 230 requires tax practitioners to use careful consideration when recommending tax positions to clients. The law dictated the manner in which tax practitioners should communicate with their clients in order to minimize confusion during conversations. Circular 230 lays out clear lines of communication between the tax practitioner and client regarding the nature of the engagement, the evaluation of facts before determining appropriate conclusions, disclosures, and potential penalties related to positions, and maintaining integrity within practice.

Circular 230 has evolved since its inception and currently makes new provisions for all tax practitioners. It outlines duties and restrictions relating to practice, sanctions for violating the regulations, and rules for disciplinary proceedings. Because tax practitioners have varying scope to practice before the IRS, the Office of Professional

Responsibility (OPR) is tasked with administering and enforcing tax practitioners' standards of practice including adherence to ethical and legal standards before the IRS as outlined in Circular 230.

The OPR has four units, Case Development and Licensure, Office of Practitioner Enrollment, Enforcement and Oversight Branch 1, and Enforcement and Oversight Branch 11. The primary functions of the former two are management of enrollment and licensure for Enrolled Agents, while the latter two focus on tax practitioner misconduct, disciplinary sanctions, settlements, and managing enrolled actuaries. Tax practitioners are censored, disciplined or disbarred from practicing before the IRS for several reasons. These reasons range from convictions for felony offenses, providing false and misleading information and representation, tax evasion, encouraging clients to violate the IRS Code, misappropriation of funds intended for the Treasury Department, bribing IRS Officers, and knowingly aiding and abetting disbarred tax practitioners to practice. Once the OPR recommends censorship, discipline, or disbarment, tax practitioners cannot correspond with the IRS, provide advice to and represent clients before the IRS, file Form 2848, Power of Attorney and Declaration of Representative, and assist anyone that constitutes practice before the IRS.

The discussion above highlights the standards of practice for tax practitioners and the role of the IRS as enforcers but there are no mentions of mechanisms to ensure clients are made aware of the infractions of tax practitioners. Moreover, how can it be established that a practitioner barred from practice does not work 'undercover' in another practice undetected? Are states and local agencies notified of practitioners who are barred from practice or have violated tax law? If the IRS is genuinely concerned with the welfare of clients, mechanisms must be in place to notify the public and more specifically the clients of unscrupulous tax practitioners.

Representing clients before IRS Appeals and Revenue Officers, signing returns, and fully or partially preparing tax returns are not the only functions of tax practitioners. As highlighted earlier, giving written advice to clients is an important component of tax practice. By filing the Form 2848, Power of Attorney and Declaration of Representative with the 1RS, clients give tax practitioners the authority to provide written advice. The basis for seeking authorization is entrenched in the notion that undisclosed positions taken by tax practitioners must have a realistic possibility of success while disclosed positions are not frivolous. In other words, tax practitioners must believe the tax treatment recommended is proper and have a reasonable basis.

Tax practitioners are constrained to make clear to clients that documents supporting positions must be in good faith and not misleading. However, there are times when tax practitioners rely in good faith without verification of information furnished by clients. Good faith suggests that tax practitioners will make reasonable inquiries into information provided by clients. Documents submitted to the IRS that contain or omit information can result in penalties for both client and tax practitioner. Penalties can be criminal and civil, including imprisonment especially in cases of negligence, intentional disregard of rules, and willful disobedience or fraud.

Another major issue with respect to giving advice to clients is conflict of interest. Previously, former IRS employees were barred for two years from providing assistance and advice to clients with whom they had a previous connection on the same matter while the tax practitioner was an employee of the Federal Government. Although, this stipulation has been removed, tax practitioners in conflict of interest situations must acquire a waiver and the tax practitioner acknowledges informed consent from the client within 30 days after the conflict. Conflict of interest between tax practitioner and client are created when the reporting standards for tax practitioners are raised above that of the client. Tax practitioners are no longer advocates, but advisors because of restriction on the types of communication allowed between tax practitioner and client.

Tax practitioners must ensure that all information disclosed by clients in good faith is reasonably verifiable. It is the full disclosure of information and verification process that creates further conflict of interest issues. Tax practitioners must choose between their personal concerns for avoiding penalties in the form of fines and sanctions by ensuring full client disclosures even when clients are averse to doing so.

The IRS has recently implemented new Preparer Tax Identification Number (PTIN) requirements to ensure that tax practitioners who substantially prepare a return should be registered with the agency. Failure to register with the IRS, pay a user fee, and have a PTIN can result in tax practitioner penalties under IRC 6695 (c). Previously, tax practitioners in place of their Social Security Number (SSN) used the optional PTIN. Currently the PTIN is mandatory for all tax practitioners irrespective of their qualifications and credentials. All tax practitioners must pay user fees and renew registration every three years. Unlike the other categories of tax practitioners, unregulated tax practitioners require compliance checks prior to renewing registration for the PTIN. The new plan to regulate unregulated tax practitioners has been stalled through legal wrangling with the IRS and unregulated practitioners. In a class action suit filed before the courts, unregulated practitioners are claiming the IRS lacks the authority to regulate tax practitioners. See *Loving v. IRS, 2013 U.S.Dist (DDC 2013)* for details of the lawsuit.

Tax practitioners Standards of Practice as outlined by Circular 230 have many implications for the tax community. Standards of Practice make clear to the tax community and more so clients the expectations of tax practitioners regardless of their varying levels of qualifications and credentials. Standards of Practice address issues of familiarity with the requirements of the IRC, and its impact on tax preparation. When tax practitioners are not adequately trained, the advice given, and positions taken on tax matters will not be sufficient to prevent errors in tax preparation. Tax practitioners have an obligation to ensure that tax advice given and positions taken reflect their knowledge, skills, and competence to provide quality service to clients. However, giving advice and taking positions on tax returns can be extensive and range from simple to complex. The tax code is in itself complex and by extension tax preparation is anything but simple even to skilled, competent and experienced tax practitioners.

While the IRS sets standards and guidelines for communicating and documenting tax advice and positions, practitioners sometimes find it difficult to comply. In practice, advice given and positions taken on tax returns by practitioners are given orally. In few cases the advice is written. When errors are made on tax returns, tax practitioners must resort to documented evidence to justify the advice given and positions taken. It is easier to retrieve written evidence but retrieving oral evidence is difficult.

One safeguard is to have both tax practitioners and clients sign the Form 2848 Power of Attorney and Declaration of Representative, which gives tax practitioners the authority to provide written advice to clients. Theoretically the safeguard sounds reasonable, but in practice tax practitioners and clients rely mostly on oral advice because clients have over time developed good rapport and client-practitioner relationships.

Ethical Hurdles

An understanding of the machinery responsible for maintaining tax preparation standards paints a quaint picture. A picture in which tax practitioners have a reasoned and ethical approach in their interactions with clients along with organizations such as the IRS and divisions such as OPR that are managing and policing policy. If this were enough to address or even understand ethical issues that confront tax practitioners every day then there would be little need for this book. The reality is the majority of tax practitioners face gray areas that impact them and their clients. The dynamics of this relationship, both positive, and negative, are generally understood in the unwritten rules of the industry but rarely touched upon in a comprehensive way.

The indiscretions of businesses and increased calls for regulation and higher ethical standards for organizational members resulted in the emergence of codes of ethics to provide guidance to members on practices that encourage ethical behavior and higher ethical standards. It must be made clear from the onset that ethical behavior is not just a matter of acting in a manner permitted by law. It necessitates building on specific practices that are acceptable and center on customs, attitudes, values, and norms within which people are expected to operate daily In some cases, an individual's ethical behavior is influenced by his or her values, work background, age, and personality.

In fact, the way individuals conceptualize right and wrong when faced with challenging moral choices is developed through formal education and preserved through continuing education. Hence,

2

education and training are critical components of initiatives designed to encourage ethical behavior and standards for the professional conduct of business.

Scholars have repeatedly alluded to the fact that some tax practitioners condone aggressive reporting during tax preparation. Professional bodies such as the American Institute of Certified Public Accountants (AICPA), National Association of Enrolled Agents (NAEA) and the IRS require that tax practitioners act with integrity to maintain public trust. In practice, many tax practitioners are faced with ethical dilemmas involving tax issues and resort to unethical activities. Tax practitioners, clients, and the IRS/Tax Agencies have varying expectations of the tax preparation process. Tax practitioners expect reliable information from clients to prepare accurate returns. Clients expect tax practitioners to provide advice and take positions to reduce tax liabilities within the ambits of tax laws. The IRS/Tax Agencies expect tax practitioners and clients to comply with the IRC.

Amidst the varying expectations of the major actors in the tax preparation process, ethical dilemmas surface when some clients are willing to adopt aggressive or even fraudulent positions based on a low probability of detection. The situation is further exacerbated when some tax practitioners are willing to go along with clients' demands for aggressive positions or fraudulent schemes.

Contemporary tax practitioners must be able to balance a host of different demands. Maintaining equilibrium is indeed difficult for tax practitioners as they seek to meet the demands of the IRC, clients, and other stakeholders in the income tax community. The challenges of income tax preparation create likelihoods for tax practitioners to be faced with ethical dilemmas during the tax preparation process. Ethical behavior in tax preparation necessitates assessing the risk of potential challenges by the IRS, State, and local tax agencies. The increased move to integrate risk management procedures into the day-to-day work of tax practitioners has emerged as a very significant issue for tax practice.

When tax practitioners take aggressive tax positions, they must be prepared for the likelihood of challenges. Aggressive positions and advice lead to "gray areas" in the tax preparation process and the possibility of audits by the IRS, State, and local tax agencies. The underlying basis for taking aggressive positions is competition. The increased demand for tax planning and preparation services has resulted in Attorneys, CPAs, EAs, RTRPs, and Unrolled Agents in nationwide tax preparation chains vying for tax business.

Tax planning is useful because it involves making use of strategies to legally minimize tax liabilities. Client's demands for lower tax liabilities or larger refunds create pressure on tax practitioners to take aggressive tax positions and give advice they know will later harm clients. This environment is comparable to a fast food chain where clients are processed as fast as possible to make accommodations for other clients in a manner similar to cars that are rushed through the drive-thru. It is during this process that mistakes are made, hasty advice is given, and unfounded tax positions are taken on tax returns that can later hurt clients and cost them financially.

Competition has also led to decrease in ethical standards as tax practitioners engage in marketing practices to obtain and retain clients. The profit motive leads tax practitioners to engage in practices that will give clients larger refunds or reduced tax liabilities. In the process of satisfying the demands of clients, many tax practitioners commit human and deliberate errors and violate tax laws. Some tax practitioners take advantage of loopholes in the tax system to take positions that can increase the tax refunds of clients. Hence the actions taken by many tax practitioners appear to be exploitative and clients are treated as means to an end in the tax preparation process. In a highly regulated industry, the practices of tax practitioners mentioned earlier raise questions of the quality of service tax practitioners are willing to offer in exchange for the compensation and to satisfy the profit motive.

Arguably, many tax practitioners do not purposefully set out to engage in practices that are outside the boundaries of widely accepted values and principles of tax preparation. There is an abundance of litigation aimed at tax practitioners that has resulted in behavior modification to ensure that consistency with the application of high ethical standards of conduct are maintained in tax preparation.

Discourse Ethics—Communicating with Clients

Discourse ethics focus on the actions of tax practitioners in relation to clients and have a practical foundation in tax preparation. The core of discourse ethics is language and communication essential to the tax practitioner-client interaction to arrive at decisions in the tax preparation process (Liddell, Cooper, Healy, & Stewart, 2010). Discourse ethics has implications for the tax preparation process because it provides a context for dialogue between tax practitioner and client when taking positions on tax returns. Moral claims to validity in communication and interaction between tax practitioners and clients is necessary if the information shared and gathered is truthful, sincere, and justified (Mingers & Walsham, 2010).

Most citizens of the U.S. spend little time focusing on taxation during the post tax season. It is understandable since clients have busy lives and should not be too occupied with performing one civic duty, filing taxes. Tax practitioners are busy pursuing other post tax season goals with little or no time to keep in touch with clients. It is during the post tax season that several tax laws are changed. When clients are not aware of the changes, no planning is done to take full advantage of the changes.

It is a common belief among many stakeholders in the tax preparation community that most people have one expectation of the tax preparation process: a refund. How much planning is needed for the refund? When we consider the post-season activities of tax practitioners and the lack of communication between practitioners and their clients, there are few opportunities to inform clients about tax law changes that will impact their tax returns the following tax season.

So who should take the initiative to keep lines of communication open during the post-season? The answer is the client as well as the practitioner. Clients have a responsibility to take charge of their personal financial activities including taxes. Clients should reach out to tax practitioners during the post tax season when major changes occur in their lives such as the birth of a child, marriage, the purchase of a home, and even an increase in salary. These activities are likely to have major effects on the tax return the next tax season. If your tax practitioner is not accessible in the post tax season you should consider seriously changing the practitioner.

I remember the case of one client who purchased her first home without consulting the tax practitioner. At the time of filing, the tax practitioner learned of the purchase. The client went into contract one week after the deadline to purchase a first home in order to get the first time home buyer credit. Who should initially take the blame here? Tax practitioners should have exit interviews with clients and use the time to inform clients of the importance to keep tax practitioners informed of likely changes during the post tax season. An exit interview was not done in the case under review.

Exit interviews allow opportunities for tax practitioners to engage clients in discourse to identify areas they may need further advice and planning. A simple question "Is there anything about your job or family that I did not ask about today?" may highlight information pertinent to the current tax return or lead to a discussion on plans the clients may have for the immediate future.

For example, a client may indicate to the tax practitioner that her five year old child is stepping up from Kindergarten to grade school, or a child is going off to college which may impact child and dependent care and college credits. A well-conducted interview can put the client at ease so they provide details about themselves likely to have tax implications. In essence, an exit interview should be done to promote positive relationships in tax preparation experience.

Tax practitioners have both moral and ethical obligations to inform clients during post tax season of changes in tax laws that will impact clients the next tax season. Tax practitioners must be proactive in passing information to clients. When tax practitioners fail to inform clients of changes in a timely manner, the practitioner is doing a disservice to clients. By the time the practitioners is doing taxes it is too late to make use of the information given during the year. What value is the information to clients during the tax season? For the tax preparation process to be meaningful to clients and practitioners, there must be direct lines of communication year-round. Tax practitioners must inform their clients of changes in tax laws and procedures. Clients must make tax practitioners aware of changes in their lives likely to impact the outcome of their tax returns. Only then will effective tax planning be possible and clients can use the advice given and information shared to their benefit.

It would be a myth to assume that conflict does not exist in the tax preparation process or between tax practitioners and clients. Tax practitioners and clients are constantly negotiating the best positions to take to reduce tax liabilities or increase refunds. Ideally, tax practitioners are expected follow the tax code in arriving at tax positions. However, in practice tax practitioners may not uphold the ideal. It is fair to clients that tax practitioners make clear their ideologies during the initial contact since both clients and practitioner have different expectations of the tax preparation process. I did not mention here tax practitioners making clear to clients the tenets of the law because it is assumed by both parties there is some legal framework in which tax preparation takes place. However since tax practitioners have varying ideologies regardless of their understanding of the IRC, there is some expectation the ideology is made known.

For example, in some major urban areas like New York and Chicago where poverty exists, clients expectation of large refunds and the existence of the Earned Income Tax Credit has put pressure on many tax practitioners to help clients get larger refunds. The practice of helping clients get larger refunds has conditioned practitioner's response to the demands of clients over time. Some tax practitioners feel that their primary role is to help clients get the maximum refund. The situation gets even more complex when practitioners perceive upholding the law may result in an unsatisfactory outcome and the possibility of losing the client. Some tax practitioners are prepared to make compromise, accommodations, and modifications to satisfy the demands of the clients.

The apparent conflict between upholding the law and ensuring that tax practitioners maintain ethical standards, clients' expectations and desires should be resolved through dialogue since both parties have a responsibility to uphold the law. The co-responsibility for upholding the law, addressing tax issues, and agreeing on tax positions can only be solved by deliberate and sustained dialogue between tax practitioners and clients mutually.

Tax practitioners should facilitate dialogue with clients to gather information pertinent to the tax preparation process. The dialogue between tax practitioners and clients must be guided by mutual respect for each other. At no point during the dialogue must either party seek to coerce each other into taking positions that could later result in infractions leading to penalties and prosecution. One tax researcher Zakeem (2008) suggested that tax practitioners must be clinicians in their advisory role. As clinicians, the tax practitioner should help clients gain deeper understanding of the tax preparation process including the tax code, practices, and procedures. Throughout the tax preparation process, tax practitioners should encourage frank dialogue to gather pertinent information that could help with tax preparation or tax planning.

Technology provides several mediums for tax practitioners and clients to communicate on tax matters during and after the tax season. The traditional medium telephone is still popular. However the use of the internet and emails are gaining popularity. Tax practitioners should consider using Skype, text messaging, and social media tools to share and gather information for tax preparation as long as clients' privacy is not compromised. Social media tools can be used to share information and receive feedback during the postseason. In the 21st century most clients turn to online communities to provide reviews on tax preparation services and bank products. Clients expect tax practitioners to establish some form of online presence where they can be kept abreast with changes taking place during the post tax season.

It is unfortunate that clients are made aware of major changes to tax laws at the time of filing. It is an unethical practice by tax practitioners to intentionally or unintentionally withhold information from clients which can later have negative effects on their tax returns. The IRS through its national trust to educate clients on changes in laws and procedures is not sufficient to meet the needs of all clients. IRS has embraced social media to help in its quest to keep the tax community abreast with developments within the agency. Major accounting and tax professional bodies such as AICPA and NAEA have also embraced social media to keep in touch with membership most of whom are tax practitioners.

It is therefore imperative that tax practitioners use various social media tools at local and grassroots levels to communicate with clients. The direct involvement from practitioners is not only ethical but adds to the credibility of the service offered to clients. Additionally, tax practitioners need to transform the way communication and dialogue is done with clients. Embracing social media, digital connections, and building an online presence to enhance practitioner-clients tax experience will boost communication and improve transparency in the conduct of the tax preparation process. Too many clients find it a nightmare to make contact with tax practitioners during the post tax season.

Facebook is a convenient and quick medium to update large number of clients with tax tips, updates in tax laws, and changes in IRS operations. Similarly, twitter is an expedient way to send brief messages to clients about filing deadlines and to get feedback on products and services. However, face-to-face rapport is likely to result in the accurate sharing and gathering of information from a privacy perspective. We must be respectful of clients comfort levels in communication and the use of social media. Not all clients are technology suave and would rather communicate using traditional mediums.

The common practice of clients "dropping off" documents at the tax office has its benefits and setbacks. Without the face-to-face pressure of sitting with clients, tax practitioners have the luxury of reading the documents presented and gaining an understanding of the clients situation without the pressure to complete the tax return because other clients are in the queue. Tax practitioners are able to focus on tax preparation at their comfort without the time constraints and pressure of long lines of clients as seen in most tax preparation chains. Tax practitioners are able to form opinions and research issues arising from the documents presented.

However, the practice of "dropping off" documents has implications for both tax practitioners and clients. Face-to-face dialogue is likely to set the tone for truthful and sincere communication between tax practitioner and clients. Tax practitioners may need to make valid determination on issues during the tax preparation process but the absence of the clients or inability to make contact at that point in time might result in the tax practitioner overlooking or omitting valuable information that can have negative outcomes for the clients. To foster dialogue in "drop off" situations, tax practitioners must set aside dedicated times to talk with the clients and resolve issues before filing the tax return.

Virtue Ethics—Does Character Really Matter?

An Aristotelian perspective of virtue ethics highlight the need for tax practitioners to be benevolent and do all that is possible in the tax preparation process to avoid harm to the client. In many respects a virtue ethicists is similar to the idealistic tax practitioner. Tax practitioners with firm and unshakable characters must prepare tax returns and give advice based on sound understanding of the tax laws, procedures, and practices. Positions taken on tax matters must be grounded in logic and not guided by emotions and the belief that tax practitioners have a social and humanitarian role to help clients alleviate poverty.

Some practitioners are of the view the tax preparation process is solely to put money in the hands of the poor during the tax season because large refunds are mostly given to low income clients who qualify for the EITC. However, the quasi-economic principle posited by some practitioners is not the reason for tax preparation and filing. Tax practitioners are cautioned to avert pursuing such routes in tax preparation. Instead, the benevolent actions of tax practitioners must focus on helping clients adhere to the tax laws while receiving the economic benefit of a refund.

The issue with tax preparation today is the client perceives the practitioner as the person who can help them to receive large sums of money with minimal effort. Within a few minutes of sitting with a tax practitioner, a client can see a transformation of his financial position giving the notion that tax practitioners are financiers. The Rapid Refund feature in tax preparation allows some clients to leave the tax office with cash in their hands and adds to the all too prevalent belief that tax practitioners help to alleviate poverty.

Some tax preparation offices have as an extension, check cashing service so that clients can realize their dreams of leaving the tax office with fast cash. Other tax preparation offices are linked to used cars dealership. For many clients, a Disney World trip, a used car, or paying off credit cards debts are all made possible through the income tax refund.

Amidst the pressure to be seen as humanitarians, many tax practitioners cross ethical boundaries. In the quest to help clients get quick money, many tax practitioners send mixed signals to clients about what their roles are in the tax preparation process. In this context, virtue ethics is relevant because it promotes the exercise of moral virtues in the business environment and tax practitioners as agents of the IRS are expected to exercise character traits or virtues that adds credibility to the tax preparation process and the industry.

The ethical behaviors posited by tax practitioners must grow from firm and unshakable characters developed through education, training, and credentialing. Tax practitioners with firm and unshakable characters add value and enhance the tax preparation process, are more likely to offer quality service, give advice, and the take positions on tax returns with maturity, carefulness, knowledge, and caution.

The larger issue in tax preparation is the lack of an objective standard to judge virtuous acts. Do the designations C.P.A, E.A, Attorney, and R.T.R.P connote competency, skills, and virtuosity? Are licensing, credentialing, and certification objective measures of virtuosity? Licensing, credentialing, and certification gives the tax practitioner the perception of being credible, skilled, and competent. Clients are also led to believe so too. However, the perception of credibility, skill, and competence may not be the case despite what tax practitioners and clients assume and does not guarantee the actions of tax practitioners are credible.

To analyze the merits or demerits of licensing, lets us focus on the basic requirement for driving a motor vehicle. Drivers are required to pass written and road tests before receiving licenses to drive on our roadways. Does licensing make a driver skilled and competent? Or does it attest to the character of the driver? The answers to both questions are no. A valid driver's license signals to other road users you have met the basic requirements to drive within some specified jurisdiction. From time to time, drivers may be asked to do defensive driving courses to help dismiss traffic tickets, reduce points from driving records, satisfy court mandated obligations, or to receive a discount from insurance companies. Whatever the need, testing is the objective measure to remain in conformity with driving on roadways or enjoy monetary benefits.

Similarly, licensing, credentialing, and certification sends signals to clients the tax practitioners have met the basic requirements to prepare tax returns. It does not mean tax practitioners are skilled and competent. Neither is it proof of virtuosity. Skills, competence, and virtuosity come with continuing education and experience in practice. Herein lays the problem for unregulated practitioners. Without licensing, credentialing, and certification it is very difficult to ascertain their skills and competencies. To say all unregulated practitioners lack skills and competencies in tax preparation is ridiculous. We must not overlook the fact that some are duly qualified in other disciplines and in business and received ethics training in their courses of studies.

However the problem of having an objective standard to judge virtuous acts is compounded by the large number of unregulated tax practitioners. It is a major issue in the U.S tax industry. One study conducted in a major U.S. city revealed that among unregulated tax practitioners, 46% had the high school diploma as the highest level of education. It is a worrying development to conceive tax preparation being done by persons with no formal training beyond high school. Some unregulated tax practitioners have Electronic Return Originators (EROs) designations given by the IRS and have their own practices with large client bases.

When coupled with the demands of clients for larger refunds and the unlikelihood of being audited, it seems as though the tax industry has a deficiency that must be addressed if credibility is to be the guiding principle in tax preparation. Credibility should stem from education, training, and a track record of sound ethical practices in the industry. When credibility stems from education, training, and a sound track record, there is a more compelling argument for upholding standards in the tax preparation process, and providing quality service.

Care Ethics—Treat Clients as Patients

The ethics of care has its origins in feminist and nursing care but is applicable in other disciplines for its increasing relevance to caring and compassion for others. Scholars in the care ethics field have repeatedly emphasized that caring and compassion for others should not be guided by adherence to a set of rules, but rather it should emanate from affection and regard for persons with whom we have caring relationships. Caring often begins with an interest in persons that expands over time through personal or professional relationships. As relationships become more concrete, a feeling of compassion and caring coupled with a commitment to help persons grow and exist.

Giving tax advice, taking tax positions, and preparing tax returns are duties that must be executed with a level of care similar to patient care in medical settings or a mother-child relationship. Tax practitioners should focus on caring, compassionate relationships and the well being of their clients. Many tax preparation chains, CPA firms, and "mom and pop" storefronts have built their businesses on the premise of offering professional services. Some tax businesses, for example, H&R Block refer to all levels of tax practitioners as "tax professionals." Tax businesses deliberately market their services as "professional." Hence there is much talk about offering professional services to clients.

Offering "professional service" is an overworked credo in the tax preparation industry. Marketing scripts are followed with precision when dealing with clients and the end result of the exercise is a satisfied customer or so it may appear. Surveys are then used to gather feedback on tax practitioners' "acting" in an attempt to further solidifying the need for self-seeking activities by the organization. In reality, choreographed acting replaces acts of care and compassion. Marketing self-seeking actions replaces actions of care, compassion, and strategies to minimize injury or risk to clients during the tax preparation process.

The care ethics brings new life to the overworked credo of professional services. Tax practitioners should focus on care and compassion for the well being of clients and meeting their needs. A recent study revealed that tax practitioners were more concerned with helping clients get the maximum refund. However, should getting clients the maximum refund be the main goal of tax preparation? The answer is no. Tax practitioners should focus on helping clients comply with tax laws. If the outcome of the tax preparation process is a refund that surpasses the expectations of clients, then it is what they deserve as long as upholding the laws was the primary focus of the engagement. Tax practitioners whose main focus is helping the clients get the maximum refund are likely to seek "gray areas" in the tax laws to ensure client gets larger refunds. Some tax practitioners take positions, give advice, and prepare tax returns in willful and reckless manners.

I can share a personal experience while working in a major tax preparation chain in New York. After completing the tax return the client was dissatisfied with the refund. The client was adamant that her tax position was similar to previous years and her refund should be higher. Not wishing to lose the client, I offered to look at her previous year tax return which she brought to the office the following day. I quickly picked up the presence of the Form 2106 which meant she used her vehicle for work related activities. I then asked her why she never told me she used her car for job related activities. She denied owning a car. Her previous tax practitioner falsified her return to give her a higher refund. Additionally, the tax return never signed by the practitioner. Hence, the tax return was designated "self-prepared" meaning the client was the preparer.

The foregoing is an illustration of the level of recklessness demonstrated by some tax practitioners. First, the tax practitioner willfully falsified the tax return by inflating expenses to give the client a larger refund. Second, the tax return was not signed by the practitioner who took no responsibility for the preparation of the tax return. Third, the tax practitioner could not be contacted because no year-round service is offered. Tax practitioners of this caliber only surface during the tax season and disappear into oblivion shortly after the close of the season.

There are other tax practitioners whose actions are not willful and deliberate, but unintentional. These tax practitioners misinterpret tax laws because of either lack of training or difficulties in interpreting tax laws. Taking aggressive positions, giving poor advice or misinterpreting tax laws has resulted in injury to many clients costing over $1,500 in understated liabilities, while resources lost by the IRS in overstated refunds exceed $2,000. Any injury to clients whether deliberate or not is malpractice.

However, the larger problem with tax practitioners in the context of care ethics emanates from two behaviors: lack of year round service and poor quality of tax preparation. It is a known fact in the tax preparation industry that a large percentage of tax practitioners are not licensed or certified to practice before the IRS. When the tax preparation season ends in April, tax practitioners who are not licensed and certified to practice before the IRS more than likely do not offer year round services. Clients who have been audited must seek the services of other licensed and certified tax practitioners to resolve the issue. Most times the engagement results in additional tax preparation fees. But what is even more alarming are the penalties and fees imposed by tax agencies if the client is in default.

Tax practitioners and clients have professional relationships that require the clients to provide reliable information and the tax practitioner is expected to provide advice and take positions that will reduce the clients tax liabilities within the scope of the IRC. The professional issue involved with care ethics is competence and the knowledge and skills that apply to standards of performance. To acquire competence, tax practitioners must pursue qualifications and credentialing to keep them informed with changes in tax laws, and the practices that improve quality of service to clients. Incompetence could harm clients resulting in infractions with severe financial penalties. To minimize the harm done to clients, tax practitioners have a duty of care to clients to ensure that relevant and reliable information is gathered during the interview phase of the tax preparation process. As information is processed and analyzed, the perceptions of tax practitioners are modified before advice is given and positions taken on the tax return.

It is not clear today if many tax practices focus on the well being of clients or the economic gains from tax preparation. The profit motives of entrepreneurs often conflict with ethical practices within businesses. To focus on the well being of clients and to exhibit high levels of care and compassion, tax practitioners must establish ethical boundaries within their own practices. The pillars of the practice should include a culture of transparency, disclosure, honesty, and the undertaking to avoid treating clients as means to an end. Clients should never be seen as objects to satisfy tax practitioners economic pursuits. Until tax practitioners see their roles as similar to medical practitioners tending to patients in an hospice, tax preparation will be viewed by many within and outside the tax community as an economic venture to satisfy the monetary pursuits of tax practitioners.

PART II

The Ideologies of Tax Practitioners

How Beliefs Can Shape Practice

Whether knowingly or not tax practitioners function within the tax community with some underlying beliefs about the tax preparation process and what their relationships with clients mean to them professionally. The beliefs held by tax practitioners in most instances guide their practice, or so it may seem. Tax practitioners are expected to adhere to standards of practice set by the IRS. In a perfect world there is no need for standards to guide practitioners. The fact that standards exist indicates that practitioners even with the most ideal intentions are likely to make choices contrary to the expectations of the standards.

Standards allow us to gauge the quality of service offered to clients. They serve as "yardsticks" in that the measure of quality has a base set by the IRS. Tax Practitioners are expected to meet or, ideally, exceed this base. The standards set by the IRS can be considered naive in some respects. Despite setting best practices for the majority of tax practitioners it assumes a certain ideology will be adhered to on the part of its audience and does not appear to take into account real world scenarios and relative experiences faced by all tax practitioners.

The major assumption is that tax practitioners are idealistic, which in practical terms means that they will all strive for perfection in all aspects and adhere to the standards that are set forth. The major weakness of IRS standards is that they cannot account for the dynamics of real world issues and ethical dilemmas. To be fair, not many standards and laws can. But the disconnect between the environment the IRS perceives and that in which actual tax preparation is conducted in is jarring. What compounds this issue is the fact that in addition to IRS guidelines laws are context dependent and can differ between states and agencies. This is not even taking into account differences in customs, values, and other conditions that adversely affect the tax practitioner.

Standards that can be considered adaptive and useful should be realistic in order for them to be applied in practice in a context dependent manner. They should be subject to change based on the dynamics of the profession. In addition, these standards should evolve based on the location of the practice because of the aforementioned dynamics. The aforementioned dynamics seems to highlight the varying levels of qualifications, credentials, and competencies of tax practitioners, their cultural backgrounds, and values and place them in different ideological groups.

Forsyth (1980) suggested that tax practitioners' variations in approaches to ethical conduct in practice may be evaluated from two approaches: idealism and relativism. However, tax preparation takes place in a real world and a realistic approach is needed if there is to be some semblance of normalcy in the evaluation of the ideologies.

What may be idealistic to an individual, group, or society may not be so in another environment. Relativism is applying the same principles to individuals, groups, or a society in another environment conditioned by the realities existing in that domain. Hence realism is needed as a safety net for tax practitioners who vary from idealism and relativism. These ideologies define the spectrum in which tax practitioners practice within the confines of the IRC.

There is a dilemma in the tax preparation industry where clients and tax practitioners alike see the IRC from varying perspectives. Some clients see adherence to ethical guidelines and federal regulations creating a philosophical dilemma between tax compliance and desire for larger refunds or reduced tax liabilities. Tax practitioners sharing similar philosophies of tax preparation may empathize with the client and even take compromising positions on tax returns to meet the client's desire. Ideally clients want a tax practitioner that will help them to avoid tax liabilities, but still do the right thing. However, not all practitioners have the same ideology of tax preparation. Some tax practitioners are realistic in their approach. They see the main purpose of the tax preparation process is to give clients the largest possible refund. Yet there are other tax practitioners who see the tax preparation process in a relativistic enclave somewhere between idealism and realism.

The dilemma intensifies when practitioners and clients ideologies conflict. Hence establishing ethical guidelines to clarify tax practitioners' judgments, responsibilities, and obligations during practice is in itself a dilemma since a host of probable factors form the basis for the varying ideologies in tax preparation. Though it is not possible in this book to address all the probable factors, it is clear that whatever the pull or push factors, clients tend to gravitate towards tax practitioners sharing similar ideologies.

The gravitation of clients to practitioners is real. Clients choose tax practitioners who will satisfy their needs consistent with their expectations of the tax preparation process and desires for larger refunds or reduced tax liabilities. If the need is a large tax refund by any means, the clients will seek out a realistic tax practitioner who will take the risk to meet the desire. If the need to get a refund with some level of caution, minor modifications and accommodations, clients are likely to seek out a relativistic tax practitioner. If the need is to have the tax return prepared that will not attract an audit and a refund is not the reason for filing, then clients will seek out the idealistic tax practitioner.

Referral is the most popular means of attracting clients to a practice. Clients are attracted to tax practitioners whose friends, relatives, or colleagues can attest to their usefulness even before engagement. Tax practitioners also use referral as a screening process to ensure clients understand and share their philosophies of tax preparation. The saying "birds of a feather flock together" is all too popular in tax preparation. Like-minded clients seek out tax practitioners who share similar ideologies only that the goals are different.

Embrace Idealist

For the idealist, tax preparation represents a process intended to uphold the tenets of the IRC and to help clients adhere to the tax laws. Although idealist are aware that the outcome of the tax preparation is either a refund or liabilities, they do not purposively set out to satisfy the expectations of clients. Idealist work objectively and ensure that outcomes, whether refunds or liabilities are the best positions for the clients. Idealism is the extent to which an individual is concerned with adhering to some set standard of practice. But more than adherence to some set standard is the care idealist have for the welfare of their clients. Highly idealistic tax practitioners feel that upholding tax laws in their practice will avoid any harm to clients.

Hence idealistic tax practitioners would rather not put themselves in positions where they must choose between the lesser of two evils when negative consequences for other people would result. Clients looking for practitioners who will prepare a tax return that is unlikely to be scrutinized by the IRS or attract an audit should settle for the idealist.

Be Watchful of Relativist

Relativists are subjective in the tax preparation process. Relativist sees client satisfaction as the primary goal in the tax preparation process. The tax preparation experience is intended to help clients get the best refund. Relativist take into consideration the expectations of the clients, their past experiences in tax preparation processes, and the added value of satisfaction. Relativists work diametrically opposite to the standards of settings, cultures, and the society at large. Tax preparation appears not to be guided by set standards but depends on which city, or state tax preparation is done. Issues of ethics and tax laws are normally circumvented. Clients are presented with rationales for circumventing laws and ethical standards to meet their desires. The IRS is often perceived as a common enemy of both the relativist and client so they can collectively pursue selfish goals.

To the relativist, upholding tax laws depends upon the nature of the situation and the individuals involved. When making decisions, the relativist is likely to weigh the circumstances more than ethical and legal implications of their actions. Clients should be watchful of practitioners who are looking for reasons to justify a refund or reduced liabilities. Practitioners who are willing to make modifications and accommodations based on the client's insistence

TERRENCE E. SIMON, PH.D.

and not on the tenets of tax laws should be viewed with caution.

Avoid Realist

Realism is a nexus between the objective world of the idealist and the subjective world of the relativist. Realists take into consideration client's real world experiences. Client's individual experiences and expectations, social and cultural norms in the locale, and the economic benefit accruing from the tax preparation experience are major considerations for the realist. However these subjective measures are processed against the IRC to determine what is best for the clients given their circumstances and experiences. Realists care less for upholding laws and weighing circumstances in the environment, but assume some risk is involved in the tax preparation process if any good results are to come from it. Clients must avoid practitioners who will give them the large refund they desire by any means. Realists are more likely to take risk to ensure clients get huge refunds or avoid liabilities regardless of the repercussions.

Will Practitioners Change Their Ideologies?

The ideologies of idealism, relativism, and realism have implications for evaluating uniformity in the application of ethical standards of conduct in tax preparation. The ideologies guiding tax practitioners are not opposites as some scholars have posited concerning the actions of individual behavior. Neither does it depict a continuum in behavior on a scale. The varying ideologies allow tax practitioners to view the IRC differently and respond to clients' desires with the same level of comfort.

Tax practitioners regardless of their qualifications and credentialing are individuals who perceive standards of practice in tax preparation differently. The perceptions of tax practitioners and their ability to comply with high ethical standards of conduct in their practices seem to be aligned with the environments in which they operate. Additionally, practitioners may never be able to change clients' ideologies of tax preparation, their desires for reduced tax liabilities or larger refunds, or even their expectations of tax practitioners. To address the ethical dilemmas in tax preparation the IRS, accounting, and tax professional bodies must ensure that ethics training and CPEs are designed to address the different ideologies to ensure uniformity in practice.

CPAs, EAs and even some RTRPs feel the purpose of tax preparation is to assist clients to uphold the tax laws in the fulfillment of their civic duty and that doing "refund taxes" is not associated with their philosophy of tax preparation. Tax practitioners as a group agree that clients have varying expectations in the tax preparation process. Whereas some clients see refunds as the only reason why tax returns are done, other clients need tax returns to be prepared so they will not be subject to scrutiny or audits. The varying expectations of clients put tax practitioners under pressure to respond within the confines of the IRC. Most low income clients expect refunds, while middle and higher income clients are more likely to have tax liabilities. There is reluctance on the part of middle and higher income clients to file their taxes. Many file extensions, or file later in the tax season as opposed to lower income clients who expect refunds. While other clients in the middle or higher income brackets are more concerned with the implications of not filing taxes on their image and characters.

Amidst the varying expectations of clients, some tax practitioners are prepared to allow clients to go to other practitioners when conflicts of expectations exist or they are not satisfied with refunds. Others are prone to compromise either because of lack of training, ignorance of the IRC, or the lure of compensation. Yet other tax practitioners are willing to make accommodations or reasonable modifications to meet the clients' desire.

PART III

The Pitfalls of Tax Practice

Challenges to Ethical Standards

The greatest challenges to tax preparation are getting clients to comply with Earned Income Tax Credits (EITC) requirements and to satisfy the requirements for the Schedule C-Profit or Loss from Business (Sole Proprietorship). The challenge with the EITC is premised on the behavior of clients who are inclined to use dependents on their income tax returns that do not meet the requirements of the IRC. Tax practitioners are required to conduct due diligence and ask questions during the interview phase of the tax preparation process to ensure that all dependents meet the residency requirements. Dependents claimed on the tax returns must have actually lived with the client for at least half or more of the tax year for which the claim for the credit is made. Additionally, current and verifiable proof of the dependent's age, relationship to client, and whether they can qualify someone else for the EITC must be obtained from all clients making claims for the EITC. Tax practitioners who fail to comply with due diligence requirements are fined $500 for each failure.

The Schedule C is used to report income and expenses from the business activities of a sole proprietor. The form is also used to report the income of statutory employees, some joint ventures and income shown on Form 1099 Miscellaneous. Persons wishing to report income in the categories above use the shortened version Schedule C EZ. The Schedule C is often seen by some as a "ball field" for the excesses of the EITC. There are many individuals who have no form of income from legitimate employment but will fabricate income and expenses, have two or three dependents and receive a refund based on the EITC. The problem with the Schedule C is the profit and loss statement forming the basis of the tax return is not audited by CPAs so widespread abuse continues because there is not enough scrutiny and due diligence carried out prior to tax preparation. For example audited accounts will go a far way to deter abuse and malpractice.

The penalties imposed for noncompliance with due diligence requirements is not enough to fully deter misreporting and evasion. Even compliant tax practitioners and clients are aware of the "audit lottery." It is a gamble of some risk that is predicated on a low detection rate. In the fiscal year 2012, 1% of all individual income tax returns (145.4 million) were audited. Some tax returns are selected for audit because the IRS receives information from third-party sources and documents such as the W2. And even smaller amount of tax returns are selected for audit because the IRS received information from its Whistleblower office, public records, and even the newspaper.

The Audit Lottery

A vast number of individual income tax returns are selected randomly through the discriminant index function (DIF). The DIF process calculates a highly randomized numeric score. Individual income tax returns with high DIF scores are more likely to be audited than returns with low DIF scores.

Tax experts Burman and Slemrod (2012) explained that tax returns selected through the DIF are done at the post processing or audit stage. The tax returns selected through the DIF do not take into account the large number of income tax returns selected for scrutiny because claims were made for refundable credits such as the EITC. In fact, 36% of all claims for refunds has as its basis the EITC. Because the EITC is claimed by low income clients, there is a belief that a greater likelihood exist for low income clients to be audited or scrutinized than their counterparts. The DIF also does not take into account an integral aspect of the tax preparation process: the tax practitioner. The score generated through the process is based on a set of variables associated with clients. There is a shortcoming of the score generated by the DIF. The tax preparation process is not a function of the clients only, but the IRS and tax practitioners are integrally a part of the process. Hence the score is biased to clients but neglects the actions of tax practitioners and their qualifications and credentials.

Theoretically, the fact that one percent of individual income tax returns are audited sounds reasonable when consideration is given to other types of clients and businesses that must be scrutinized if the system is to appear objective. However, the audit rate of one percent allows tax practitioners to engage in practices of overstating expenses associated with credits and deductions. Even well intentioned tax practitioners could be pressured into playing such odds despite the potential repercussions. In their research, Bolt-Lee and Moody (2009) found that client pressure practitioners to play the "audit lottery" because of low detection rates.

The policy of the IRS to audit 1% of all income tax returns annually should be revisited. Many tax practitioners believe that it opens the floodgate for malpractice by unscrupulous tax practitioners. There is greater need for enforcement and compliance when consideration is given to the large percentage of unregulated tax practitioners. Some tax practitioners and other stakeholders in the tax community alike feel that a strengthened audit department will "level" the playing field and remove the threat of loss of business to licensed/ certified practitioners from unscrupulous practitioners. The slim chance of an audit pushes tax practitioners to satisfy clients' desire for larger refunds or reduced tax liabilities.

The larger issue with the current policy is the belief that the IRS needs to take a more realistic approach to auditing. Audits should be deliberate rather than random following some objective selection process that includes variables associated with tax practitioners such as education, training, and credentialing. A more reasonable audit rate of 7% to 10% will serve as a greater deterrence to practitioners engaging in unscrupulous practices because of the higher chance of detection.

Many tax practitioners agree there were instances when they felt pressured by clients to take risk because of the low possibility of detection. The issue of client pressure is real. Experts researchers in tax preparation such as Bolt-Lee and Moody (2009) allude to the levels of pressure tax practitioners are exposed to during the tax preparation process. Many practitioners however fell short of saying whether they yield to clients' insistence on larger refunds / reduced liabilities although most practitioners agree they refused to succumb to the pressures of clients regardless of the loss of business.

It comes as no surprise that many practitioners do not wish to discuss whether they yielded or not to the pressures of some clients. Research on the subject reveals that despite the reticence of some practitioners, some are yielding to pressure to take aggressive positions and they are failing to perform sufficient due diligence during tax preparation. Other tax practitioners allow clients to take positions that are not supported by documentable evidence to support claims for credit or deductions such as the EITC, Dependent Care Credit, Education Credit, and Tuition Deduction.

Researchers such as myself and Raskolnikov (2006) suggested that tax practitioners could avert such pressure by attending training in ethics. It follows that ethics training is likely to help tax practitioners avoid client pressure to take unwarranted positions by establishing ethical guidelines to ensure that judgment, responsibility, obligations and the culture of tax preparation could be geared towards adding value to clients. This allows tax practitioners to avoid pressure through an improved climate of compliance.

PART IV

Preventing Malpractice

Training and Education

The training and education of tax practitioners are pivotal in their response to ethical issues in the tax preparation process. Training and education are instructor-led, content-based interventions that can lead to desired changes in behavior of tax practitioners. Research has shown that training and education are the primary means of reducing the likelihood of error, and serves as a means of altering and improving performance. In order to meet the challenges of income tax preparation the experience, the training received and knowledge acquired by tax practitioners are extremely relevant.

This is not lost on many scholars and, according to Hill (2011), those practitioners who have reached the highest of skill to be competent practitioners should be distinguished from individuals who have not. This happens to some extent as the IRS differentiates between those tax practitioners who have limited scope to practice and represent clients before the IRS (Cords, 2009). A potential problem is the matter of expectations, as tax practitioners are expected to pursue training that will result in high levels of competence, knowledge, skills, and proficiency commensurate with the expectation of the tax preparation profession (Oh & Lim, 2011).

Coetzee and Oberholzer (2009) observed that training in accounting, and taxation is not adequate to produce skilled, knowledgeable, and competent tax practitioners because most tax education curricula focus on memorizing the IRC with little allowance for applying the tenets of the tax laws in practical situations. Therein lies the central problem. When the education is insufficient to produce competent professionals the industry is eroded at its very foundation. Effective income tax training must result in providing tax practitioners with the requisite skills and knowledge to assist clients with the most trusted advice.

Some practitioners are of the view that unregulated tax practitioners merely prepare taxes for the monetary gains but care little about the clients' welfare. Even if there are trained by tax preparation chains including H&R Block, Liberty Tax Service or Jackson-Hewett the quality of work is still substandard because many unregulated tax practitioners do not fully understand the IRC to apply it in varying situations when facing clients. When faced by pressure from clients to take aggressive positions, they succumb easily sometimes intentionally, but in other circumstances it mere ignorance.

For example, many tax practitioners inflate deductions on the Schedule A to reduce tax liabilities and increase the tax refunds. If the practice was not unscrupulous in itself, how can a tax practitioner explain itemizing 60% of a client's income? How practical is it to take such a position? How could the client survive on 40% of his or her income? Situations like the one discussed above give a glimpse of the level of unprofessional conduct existing in the U.S tax industry. Tax practitioners' ignorance of the IRC has injured clients costing thousands to the IRS including penalties and interest. In a market where 54% of the tax practitioners are unregulated with a much smaller percentage of licensed or certified, many clients are exploited, and a culture of substandard work is encouraged.

Some may argue that training alone can help practitioners avoid the pressures from clients to get them large refunds. However, when we consider that unregulated practitioners are not required to do any form of ethics training to maintain their practice it makes it easier for them to succumb to the pressures of unscrupulous clients who are prepared to ignore tax laws to gain larger tax refunds or reduce tax liabilities. Unregulated tax practitioners do not feel pressured or obligated to perform to some set standard because of non affiliation to professional bodies such as the AICPA. In essence, unregulated tax practitioners have little to lose when clients are harmed in the tax preparation process. There is no risk of losing a license and very little chance of being caught in malpractice because unregulated tax practitioners very seldom sign tax returns they prepare. Many returns prepared by unregulated tax practitioners are designated "self-prepared."

Even if tax practitioners are trained in ethics, it may not be sufficient to curb malpractice in tax preparation. Skills and competence in tax preparation must stem from education supplemented by training. The high incidence of unregulated tax practitioners with the high school diploma as the basis for practicing is a cause for concern among practitioners. If the regulators of the industry allow tax practitioners with low levels of education to practice regardless of tax and ethics training received, its spells disaster for the U.S tax industry. In New York State, CPAs are required to do four hours of ethics training once every three years. The training requirements of CPAs may differ from state to state. On the other hand, EAs are required to do two hours of ethics training annually.

It is the general feelings of many tax practitioners who were educated outside of the U.S. that the U.S has an excellent framework and good mechanisms in place for tax preparation. Training and practice outside of the US is different. In some countries it is not a civic or constitutional duty of citizens to file taxes annually. Because there are no pressures to file taxes annually, the pressures of compliance is not a major issue to tax practitioners most of whom are certified or chartered accountants affiliated to professional bodies with varying ethical standards for practice.

The US tax industry seems to have higher levels of requirements in place to ensure compliance with standards of practice in tax preparation than most countries. However, some tax practitioners who received ethics training and education outside of the US feel the local industry does an effective job of producing competent and ethical practitioners.

In addition to competency, Cords (2009) suggested that tax practitioners need training to ensure that clients are not harmed when advice and tax positions are given during income tax preparation resulting in understatement of tax liabilities, and overstatement of refunds. Some tax practitioners are trained in taxation over short durations in "crash" courses lasting from one week to three months. This type of training affects the tax practitioner's ability to interpret the requirements of the IRC. More intensive training such as EA's certification, licensing, and continuing professional education tailored to address a deeper understanding of the IRC and ethics result in tax practitioners having greater awareness of the requirements of the IRC.

The greater issue with tax practitioner's training has to do with the aggressive positions they are willing to take when dealing with tax issues. Attorneys, CPAs, and EAs are perceived as having greater tax expertise than RTRPs and unregulated tax practitioners (Schmidt, 2001). Hence, there are greater expectations of tax practitioners with credentials and licenses to provide aggressive tax advising. The aggressiveness is not limited to tax preparation, tax planning, and tax advising, but in advocating their services.

The AICPA has been advocating that CPAs should differentiate themselves from other tax practitioners by highlighting their credentials, commitment to ethical standards, pursuit of continuing professional education requirements, and their availability and accessibility year-round. These are excellent reasons for advocating the accreditation divide. EAs should also distinguish themselves from other tax practitioners because their certification is national unlike CPAs who are licensed to operate within their states of residence or the jurisdiction covering their licenses.

The Competent Tax Practioner

Tax practitioner's availability and year-round accessibility is linked to their qualifications and credentials, and their ability to practice before the IRS. Attorneys, CPAs, and EAs can offer year-round services to clients because they are qualified and licensed to make representation to tax agencies on tax issues such as audit representation, payment arrangements for tax liabilities, and serving as Power of Attorneys for clients. Holtzman (2004) explained that licensed and certified tax practitioners offer year round service because they must respond or react to changes in regulations and statutes that affect clients. unregulated tax practitioners do not offer year-round services because they see clients as means to an end (Altman, 2007).

The differentiation of tax practitioners by qualification and credentials is intended to send messages to clients that licensed and certified tax practitioners offer quality services. Quality service does not guarantee tax preparation free of errors. However, because licensed and certified tax practitioners are accountable for their actions to the IRS, and licensing and credentialing bodies, higher standards and quality professional service in tax preparation are expected (Elgin, 2008; "American Institute of Certified Public Accountants," 2009).

A recent study conducted in New York City revealed that many tax practitioners have the minimum qualifications to prepare tax returns. Even though many of the practitioners are exposed to continuing education related to tax practice, the concern is whether the minimum training and education received is enough to help the tax practitioners uphold ethical standards in their practices.

The dilemma surfacing with providing quality tax preparation service year round is impacted by the large number of unregulated tax practitioners who cannot represent clients before the IRS whether during or after the tax season ends. Can unregulated tax practitioners have reputable practices that offer quality service? Many stakeholders in the tax community will differ with the position since lack of training is likely to impact tax practitioners' ability to interpret tax laws, some of which are all too complex. Additionally, unregulated tax practitioners non-affiliation with professional bodies and agencies can raise concerns of their ethical conduct in practice and whether tax practitioners not authorized to practice before the IRS are prone to malpractice. Researchers in the tax preparation field Hill (2009), Altman (2007), and Bauman and Mantzke (2004) explained that unregulated tax practitioners can do more harm than good to clients and raises questions about their overall competence as tax practitioners.

The discussion on tax practitioners training and providing quality service will be replete with misconceptions if the issue of "self-prepared" is avoided. The IRS process millions of self-prepared tax returns annually. Individuals filing self prepared tax returns may or may not have any training in tax preparation, but use tax software to prepare their tax returns. The "self-prepared" category of tax practitioners are not required to be licensed or certified. It therefore seems confusing that individuals preparing their own taxes are not required to show some level of skill and competence. Shouldn't there be some standard in place for self-prepared tax returns? Shouldn't individuals in the "self-prepared" category receive some form of training in ethics to ensure they comply with the

IRC and held accountable for their actions? How do we evaluate ignorance of the tax laws versus deliberate, intentional acts to defraud the IRS? It may be simple to finger a tax practitioner for malpractice but harder to prove in the case of a "self prepared" tax return.

EPILOGUE

The tax preparation process is very intricate, risky at times, but rewarding especially to tax practitioners. The tax practitioners' job is to create a level of comfort and trust with clients. However, the ethical dilemmas faced by tax practitioners has continually challenged the very principles and standards of conduct, and ethical behavior in the US tax industry while highlighting policy issues. Education and training is important and tax practitioners should take steps to keep abreast with new developments in the tax industry. Moreover, ethics training designed to capture the varying ideologies of tax practitioners is warranted at this juncture. The one size fits all approach currently used in ethics training will not benefit tax practitioners who regardless of standards of practice in place will be guided in tax preparation by their ideologies.

The IRS has annual nationwide tax forums to provide tax practitioners with information and resources to assist in their professional development. The benefits of continuing professional education to tax practitioners will result in better quality service to clients who crave for higher quality tax preparation experience.

The large number of unregulated tax practitioners and the current audit rate of 1% should be addressed by Congress because the current policy affects the very core of the tax preparation industry. However, the larger issue is consumer rights. Clients are the real victims of malpractice. The financial cost including penalties and interest affects clients and not practitioners. Stronger consumer advocacy is one way of pressuring the government to intervene in regulating tax practitioners.

Licensed and certified tax practitioners are not the best advocates for regulation because they are vying for market share with unregulated tax practitioners who represent the largest group of tax practitioners in the US actually doubling that of CPAs. The motives of licensed and certified tax practitioners for regulation would always be questioned by some practitioners and researchers in the field of ethics and tax preparation. We may never know the real reason behind the push for regulation, whether it is genuine care for clients or increased monetary gains for licensed and certified tax practitioners.

REFERENCES

Altman, M. (2007). The decomposition of the corporate body: What Kant cannot contribute to business ethics. *Journal of Business Ethics, 74*(3), 253-266.

American Institute of Certified Public Accountants. (2009). *Statement on standards for tax services No. 6, knowledge of error: Return preparation and administrative proceedings*. Retrieved on 02/18/2012 from www.aicpa.org/ . . . /Tax/./ StandardsEthics.

Bauman, C., & Mantzke, K. (2004). An education and enforcement approach to dealing with unscrupulous tax preparers. *ATA Journal of Legal Tax Research, 249*-60.

Bolt-Lee, C., & Moody, J. (2009). Change in the taxpayer-tax preparer relationship: The effects of circular. *Journal of Legal, Ethical & Regulatory Issues, 12*(1), 15-25.

Burman, L.E., & Slemrod, J. (2012). *Taxes in America: What everyone needs to know.* New York, NY: Oxford University Press.

Coetzee, S., & Oberholzer, R. (2009). The tax knowledge of South African trainee accountants: A survey of the perceptions of training officers in public practice. *Accounting Education, 18*(4/5), 421-441.

Cords, D. (2009). Paid tax preparers, used car dealers, refund anticipation loans, and the earned income credit: The need to regulate tax return preparers and provide more free alternatives. *Case Western Reserve Law Review, 59*(2), 351-391.

Elgin, E. (2008). Circular 230: Final amendments reflect a balanced approach. *Journal of Tax Practice & Procedure, 10*(1), 25-63.

Forsyth, D. R. (1980). Taxonomy of ethical ideologies. *Journal of Personality and Social Psychology 39*, 175-184.

Hill, C. (2009). Celebrating a decade of tax controversy observations and insights. *Journal of Tax Practice & Procedure, 11*(2), 17-20.

Holtzman, Y. (2004). The transformation of the accounting profession in the United States: From information processing to strategic business advising. *The Journal of Management Development, 23*(10), 949-961.

Liddell, D. L., Cooper, D. L., Healy, M. A., & Stewart, D. (2010). Ethical elders: Campus role models for moral development. *About Campus, 15*(1), 11-17.

Mingers, J., & Walsham, G. (2010). Toward ethical information systems: The contribution of discourse ethics. *MIS Quarterly, 34*(4), 833-854.

Oh, T. H., & Lim, M. S. (2011). Intention of tax non-compliance-examine the gaps. *International Journal of Business and Social Science, 2*(7), 1-6.

Raskolnikov, A. (2006). Crime and punishment in taxation: Deceit, deterrence, and the self-adjusting penalty. *Columbia Law Review,106*(3), 569-642.

Schmidt, D.R. (2001). The prospects of taxpayer agreement with aggressive tax advice. *Journal of Economic Psychology, 22*, 157-172.

Zakhem, A. (2008). Stakeholder management capability: A discourse—theoretical approach. *Journal of Business Ethics, 79*(4), 395-405.